HONEY POT PR.

The People of St. Paul's

The Last 100 Years

Elizabeth Jerram

2012

An attempt to record something of what people remember about their involvement in life at St. Paul's, Weston-super-Mare over the last 100 years.

Published by Honey Pot Press
2 The Dell, Worle
BS22 9LZ
www.honey-pot-press.co.uk

January 2013

Copyright © Elizabeth Jerram 2013
The Author asserts the moral right to be
identified as the author of this work.
ISBN: 978-0-9569752-8-7

I should like to record my grateful thanks to all those who have contributed to this book in any way.   Without their efforts to 'remember' there would be no book.

Cover photographs taken by Ian Jerram

On July 22nd 2012, at the 9.30 service, we followed almost exactly (give or take a bishop or two!) the form of service used in 1911 when the foundation stone was laid for a new church building. This building replaced the temporary 'tin church' built on land donated for the purpose by Rebecca Davies in memory of her husband.

In 1997, Gordon Pratt spent lots of time and energy researching and writing a very full and detailed history of the church, including at the end of his book some 'memories' from members of the congregation at that time, (sadly the book was not published until just after Gordon's death although he did see it in its first printed form). These memories gave me the idea for a new book to celebrate the 100 years since the consecration of the present building, - a book about the people of St Paul's and the momentous changes they have lived through, accepted and embraced, - changes and experiences which have perhaps led to St Paul's becoming the vibrant and lively centre of worship that it is today.

St Paul's has grown from one to five congregations happily co-existing under one roof and I hope this little book might record something of what people remember about their involvement in what I think has always been a very special, very welcoming community. It is, today, a much more diverse community and there is so much going on here, catering for people with different needs, different interests and different ways of worshipping that it has outgrown the present buildings.

But what is it about St Paul's that has made it so special? Why has it been so blessed through the years with congregations which seem to have embraced quite drastic changes even when they sometimes felt very uneasy about them?

Beginnings

To start to find the answers to these questions perhaps we need to go back to the very beginning, to 1897 when the Bishop of the diocese "solemnly dedicated the iron building as it was then, to the service of God". He told the congregation that this church was placed here to see if it was wanted, and the test of its being wanted was that at the end of two years it should be self supporting. "Failing the accomplishment of that, it was to be removed." The remarkable man who was vicar of St Paul's at that time, **Reverend T.H.S. Polehampton** and his congregation took the Bishop's advice on board and ran with it! Like the earliest Christians they responded to God's challenge so that Reverend Polehampton was moved to comment (when St Paul's had been

Rev. T. H. S. Polehampton

up and running for not two but seven years), how much the work of the church was, *"handicapped and crippled beyond all measure through want of accommodation."*

Does this situation sound familiar?

Rev. Polehampton went on to address his congregation on the importance of 'unity' to a church.

"I thank you all for your loyal, cordial and hearty co-operation as choir, as a congregation and as church officials. There can be no more striking illustration of the importance of unity, for a clergyman is useless without a choir and a choir useless without a clergyman and without a congregation both are useless and unless all pull together and pull the same way they can accomplish nothing".

Unity, he stressed should ever mark their actions and plans, *"and might we so continue to work together for the glory of God and for the extension of His Church militant here on earth, that in His mercy He might deem us worthy to be members of His Church triumphant in Heaven."*

A remarkable man indeed was this first vicar of St Paul's. He was Vicar of the 'tin church' which was the first church on the site in 1897. It soon had to be extended and by 1904 the congregation numbered over 1000. There were 40 men and boys in the choir and 177 children in the Sunday School. The Whitecross Hall was opened in Rev Polehampton's time to be used for the Sunday School and for social activities.

Gordon says about him, that *"Probably no priest ever lived on more intimate terms with his congregation and fellow residents,"* and indeed this involved opening up his home for parish functions since there was no church hall until the Whitecross Hall was opened in 1908.

"With the power of great faith and the will and support of his parishioners, his dream of the stone church was near to becoming a reality," but sadly he was not to see it come to fruition as he died suddenly at the age of fifty, in the summer of 1909. He had though left behind the legacy of a unified, welcoming church, a generous congregation and a tradition for looking out beyond the church walls to care for the whole community. It is significant that the whole town mourned his passing.

Before the stone church became a reality, St Paul's acquired a building at the junction of Clifton Road and Walliscote Road which when converted, "as funds allowed," became the Whitecross Hall and it would serve the work of the church and the whole community for the next sixty years. Gordon Pratt comments that this hall, *"was the social meeting place of the period,"* and *"was constantly in use for either St Paul's social and fund-raising events or being used by other organisations."* Thus, a tradition of hospitality was being established and it is obvious from some of the events Gordon outlines that the hall *"was a very busy place."*

INTERIOR OF ST. PAUL'S CHURCH, WESTON-SUPER-MARE

The stone church, although not entirely completed, was consecrated on St Andrew's Day, 30th November, 1912. The Dean of Wells preached the sermon and pointed out that the people were that day raising a new witness to their Christian faith. Nor did the witness end with those who joined in the service that day. Indeed that was only the beginning.

The church would stand in the midst of the habitations of men as a permanent sign of the living God.

It was meant for His glory, it would be used for His worship.

He added, however, that it was the existence of the church and not its dignity or its costliness that was the essential element of that witness. He spoke to them of the importance of the work of overseas mission and of the value of tiny mission churches in Australia (!)

(I wonder what he would have thought of two intrepid Australians of today, Brian and Ali Champness, 'doing things' the other way round and coming here to St Paul's to lead our Children's Church! And I wonder how he would have reacted to the amazing 'Aussie Bible'?)

This new church, the Dean added, was a witness to the devotion of the people who had built it, the consecration which had hallowed it and the worship offered in it. He told the congregation they must live their lives, *"in devotion to Christ, open to the Spirit, and in worship of the Father"*.

The Bishop of Bath and Wells then spoke of the joy of not only consecrating the church that day but also the Whitecross Hall, formerly a Baptist church, to be used for the Sunday School which was an indication of the way the late vicar, Rev Polehampton, was always looking ahead. He spoke too of the financial need not to be content to simply live upon what their predecessors might have done. They were going to endeavour to help themselves and would begin to experience a new life in the church.

The ordinary people of the church would have a much greater role to play in the future of the church in the years to come (prophetic words indeed).

Rev. D. Lloyd

Times would not be easy for the vicar, Rev D. Lloyd, (who followed Reverend T. H. S. Polehampton) and his congregation, for within two years of the consecration the country was thrust into the horror and devastation of 'The Great War.' Nearby Clarence Park became a training ground for soldiers and lots of the young men of the parish left home to join the forces. Many did not of course return and their names are recorded in the church, on a board beneath the west window and behind the font. (We 'flower ladies' always read out the names of these

'people of St Paul's' when decorating the font for Remembrance Day.)

Congregations were large in the war years and were swelled by children from several private boarding schools for whom church attendance was compulsory. Gordon records the ongoing generosity of the congregation in their charitable giving and describes how, in 1927, the building was finally completed.

Preb. J. E. S. Harrison

The church had obviously provided spiritual comfort for the community in the First World War, but harder times still were approaching when under the leadership of Prebendary Harrison (who took over from Rev Norris in 1936) the church and the town would face danger, damage and death as a result of World War 2.

4000 young evacuees from the London area were sent to Weston at the beginning of the Second World War and it is reported that many of them were confirmed at the Church. It is also reported that many of them returned home to London, their families thinking that Weston was too dangerous!

The town certainly suffered a great deal of bomb damage in the war and on 4th January, 1941, *"3000 incendiary bombs and some high explosives,"* fell on the town. The incendiaries directly hit St Paul's and the central nave area of the church was devastated. St Andrew's Chapel seems to have escaped with scorching only but the Whitecross Hall was also badly damaged in the raid.

Bomb damage, Jan 4th 1941

Once again vicar and congregation would have to rise above terrible adversity and it would be sixteen years before the building was fully restored. But a church is more than just a building and this church carried on. (Perhaps in the spirit which enabled today's congregations to carry on through the cold days of last winter without heating!) The wartime congregation carried on by holding services in the Grammar School, then in the specially adapted south aisle of the church and later, when it had been restored, in the Whitecross Hall so that work could be completed on the church building.

South Aisle used during restoration

The church would not be fully restored for some time. Indeed it was not until 1957, after years of fund-raising and planning that the new building would be dedicated by the Bishop. The much loved reredos representing the Last Supper and the beautiful pulpit were restored and cleaned and the original chairs were replaced with costly pews but the ornate wooden choir screen was not replaced, giving more openness and light to the building. There are incidentally, places in the church and particularly in St Andrew's chapel where the scorched wood was left in place, perhaps to remind people of all the church went through.

The Reverend Harrison was shortly to write:

'Resurgat'

It shall arise – and lovelier still
Even than it was before;
With courage, faith – with heart and will,
We shall God's house restore;
Though man may wreck his deadliest ill,
His vilest deeds outpour,
He never can the spirit kill –
This liveth ever more!
Come then, join hands, be brave, and play the part –
Give God the praise and honour due,
To Him be faithful, loyal, true –
Results are sure if in His hands,
He knows, He cares, He understands.

300 WAIT DISAPPOINTEDLY OUTSIDE WHILE...
1,000 See Rebuilt Church Consecrated at Weston

OVER 1,000 people thronged the newly re-built St. Paul's Church at Weston-super-Mare to overflowing last night, and hundreds were unable to gain admission to see the Bishop of Bath and Wells, Dr. W. H. Bradfield, consecrate it.

Over half an hour before the service was due to start the only seats available in the church were those reserved for the Mayor and Mayoress of Weston, Coun. Lt.-Col. G. C. G. Grey and Coun. Mrs. M. J. Grey, and Borough Council members and officials.

Outside the west doors slow-moving queues had halted in the evening sunshine by 6.30 p.m. and a policeman had to clear an avenue in the waiting throng by the door to make way for the Bishop to approach the west door and claim traditional entry by striking three times on the panel with his crosier.

The procession, headed by the Bishop and his chaplain, Preb. G. W. Battersby, Rector of Weston, then entered the church with the choir and clergy.

No sooner had the procession entered than a throng of people surged forward only to be halted by a policeman who assisted sidesmen in closing the door.

Before the service started Preb. J. E. S. Harrison, Vicar of St. Paul's, apologised to the crowd outside and explained that the church was filled to capacity and that extra seats had already been provided in available spaces in the aisles.

"We should like to find room for you all—but there it is," he told the throng by the main doors.

The Bishop was accompanied by the Ven. H. B Salmon, Archdeacon of Wells, and Preb. R. S Urch, of the Church of the Good Shepherd, daughter church of St. Paul's.

Among the 300 or so people who failed to find seats or standing room in the church was a number of invitation ticket-holders, including Press representatives.

Copies of the order of service were handed to many of the disappointed people who waited in the queues and finally saw the doors closed.

THE BISHOP at the west door before the start of the service.

THE VICAR, Preb. J. E. S. Harrison, apologises to some of the crowd of over 300 who were unable to get in for the service.

6/6/57

PRECEDED BY THE MACE, the Mayor and Mayoress. Lt.-Col. G. C. G. Grey and Coun. Mrs. M. J. Grey, walk in procession with the Vicar, Preb. J. E. S. Harrison, and the Rector of Weston, Rev. G. W. Battersby.

Not all the people of St. Paul's got in!

Left: The restored Church, with pews!

Bottom Left: The original Church without pews!

THE OFFICE FOR THE

Consecration

of

S. Paul's Church

Weston-super-Mare

by the Right Reverend
WILLIAM, LORD BISHOP OF BATH AND WELLS

on

WEDNESDAY, JUNE 5th, 1957
at 7 p.m.

Not many years after the rededication of the church, Preb. Harrison died and his place was taken by Rev Vivian Payne, a Welshman.

Rev. Vivian Payne

Viv Payne retired in 1981. During his time our daughter church, the church of the Good Shepherd, built in 1923 was closed, causing great sadness to those people who had worshipped there. During Rev Payne's time also, the Whitecross Hall was sold and a new hall built on the same site as the church. It opened with much rejoicing in 1971.

Rev Noel McKittrick followed Vivian Payne, with his wife, Christa, who became organist and choir-mistress. Noel preached some memorable sermons, introduced us to some interesting speakers, and visited a great number of the houses in the parish and we were all sad to lose Christa's leadership of the choir and her encouragement of the children, when Noel retired in 1992.

Rev. Noel McKittrick

Then, after an interregnum during which John Neville took the reins with confidence and obvious enjoyment, Huw Davies and his family came to us and St Paul's would never be the same again.

Rev. Huw Davies and family meet the Bishop of Taunton

Huw dragged us – (with a little kicking and screaming, but no real unpleasantness I think), into the modern world. The church was decorated, (thanks to a generous bequest from Ity Spearing), the pews were taken out, a pink carpet was laid and the choir vestry was converted into the church office, presided over by Ian Todd, without whom we all think that things would probably grind to a halt. (All that and he also does very good sermons!) Most importantly, St Paul's was introduced to the Alpha Course which is a non-threatening introduction to Christianity, through which many people have found faith, and a second service, at eleven o'clock was introduced. The more relaxed style of worship at this service has attracted many new people to the church.

Jos Holder remembers being part of the 'changes'. She says of that time:

"A few months before we started the second service, Anna (Huw's wife) invited Sian, Gerry Cromwell, Ian Jerram and myself to Sian's house for a music session and although none of us knew the reason for this, it was actually the start of the Music Group. We had our own instruments and there was no sound box in the church. This was the way we played for several months, and then someone bought the church a keyboard. I used to hide behind a pillar when I was playing it but when the church was revamped Huw told me I would no longer be able to do this as the front of the church was changing. He even showed me a spotlight which he called 'Jos's light' and told me I could no longer hide!"

Huw and his family left St Paul's in 2005 and no-one was surprised, but all were delighted, when his place was taken by Rev Andrew Alden. Andrew's vision for the church has built on the changes made by Huw and we now have not two but five congregations worshipping here at St Paul's! There are also ambitious plans to extend the church buildings to provide room for all that now goes on here.

The church is the people

From this very potted history it is obvious that our church has lived and grown through turbulent times. So what do the people who lived through the turbulence remember? How were they affected by the changes – some imposed from outside, as with two world wars, some cultural changes, affecting the way people regarded the church and some changes inside the church involving new styles of worship?

A good place to look for early memories is Gordon Pratt's book in his 'Time to Remember'. Most, if not all of the people whose memories are included there are no longer with us but their words give us vivid glimpses, especially of Rev Polehampton. Gordon recorded their memories in 1997.

Miss Dorothy May Williams (aged 100) tells that her brother was assistant organist at both the churches (St Paul's and the Good Shepherd). She attended Rossholme School and was very fond of Rev. Polehampton and his wife. She says that all sorts of things used to happen at church and there were lots of activities at the Whitecross Hall. (I wonder what sort of 'things' she meant!)

Mrs Edith Saltford's memories are a little more detailed. She loved music and was organist at the Good Shepherd Church. She used to play Handel on the organ and Chopin on the piano. There was no Mothers' Union then but there was a Sewing Circle and the church was very friendly and happy.

Mrs Irene Martin (95) has lots to tell. Her mother and father were confirmed in the 'tin church'. She was rather frightened of Rev Polehampton's voice although she thought he was wonderful and always 'spoke well'. She felt he never really died, that his presence was still in the church. Rev Lloyd had eight children, the first three born on the same day three years running! The angels' heads in the nave, she says, were believed to be based on his children. She was a Sunday School teacher at the age of eighteen and remembers the Whitecross Hall being 'full of kids' and that there were about 20 teachers.

Church seats then were, 'One guinea for an outside seat and half a guinea for an inside seat'. (I presume this was the cost of having your own reserved seat.)

Mrs Martin's father was church auditor and her mother was in the Mother's Union and did the flowers. She remembers Sunday School charabanc trips to the Exmoor hills, Whitecross Hall for events and stalls in Clarence Park. She remembers too how Rev Polehampton took the trouble to make fires and dinners for needy people and has memories of services being conducted at the Grammar School when the church was bombed.

Mrs Doris Bindon (97) tells how her mother and father were married at Emmanuel Church by Rev Polehampton because the 'tin church' was not licensed for marriages. Rev Norris was, because of deafness, not a good speaker. She remembers him waving at people at a distance and that he had a dog called Roy (!) She was involved in the yearly Sale of Work and would organise the Bran Tub. She remembers the concerts in the Whitecross Hall and the sale of 'penny sheets' for church and organ funds. She speaks of Sunday School trips to Portishead and Clevedon on the Light Railway which was very slow and sometimes even stopped.! She also remembers the talented Dimoline family and Rev Harrison who wrote hymns and poetry. He was very clever and his wife, a Lady, died first.

Mrs Bindon was married in the 'side aisle', served on the PCC and ran the Brownie pack for 36 years. She attended the Good Shepherd Church and enjoyed its parties (it was 2 shillings and sixpence for Harvest Supper and entertainment). She was very disappointed at the closure of the Good Shepherd Church since it was only really its hall that was unsafe.

Mr Keith Dimoline's family were involved in the very early fund-raising for the church. The famous 'Dimo' pantomimes were held at the Knightstone Theatre. He joined the choir aged eight and would jump over the rear garden wall of the family house straight into the church grounds. Choir had 14 men and 24 boys but no women. He was gifted with a good solo voice and performed many times, becoming head choir boy, responsible for boys' appearances, i.e. straight ties, clean shoes, tidy dress. He attended St Paul's on the cold morning after it was bombed and witnessed the destruction. He remembers the Scout group under Stoker White, a very kind and godly man.

Ity Spearing (92) died in 1995, having lived all her life in the parish, her parents keeping a Bed and Breakfast house on Beach Road in the early years of the century. Ity, her brother Ron and sister Audrey were brought up in St Paul's and she had fond memories of the old 'tin church' where she was baptised and the choir of which Ron was a staunch member in the 1920's/30's.

It was as a result of a very generous legacy from Ity that the redecoration of the church could go ahead so boldly in 1997. Wonderful memories aren't they? And we have Gordon Pratt to thank for rescuing them before they were no longer available.

Modern Memories

I've spoken to lots of people who go to the nine thirty service and obviously there is no longer anyone who can remember Rev. Polehampton but lots of people remember him by name and Liz Cromwell knew some members of his family. He seems to have been quite a character and and well known throughout the town.

Derek and Liz Cromwell shared quite a few early memories with me. Derek's father came to Weston from Birmingham in 1898 and eventually owned a Garage on Devonshire Road. Derek remembers his mother taking him and his brother to St Paul's Church where they had 'special' seats five or six rows from the front. In those days parishioners could 'buy' a seat for a year for £5-00. (Don't even think about it, Andrew!) If you were late though, your seat would be given to someone else, so it was common to see latecomers tearing up the road to make sure they got their seat!

Both Liz and Derek remember the church being bombed on January 4, 1941.

As a small child Liz witnessed the immediate effects of the bombing. She could see smoke and flames leaping into the sky and remembers being very frightened. Derek remembers the side aisles being blocked off from the nave by a local builder and services eventually being held in the south aisle leading to St Andrew's Chapel.

The north aisle became a temporary mortuary during the war years, to be used when needed for casualties. Derek and Liz remember American troops being in the town, training in the local parks and being billeted in hotels near St Paul's. If there was a raid they had to rush to the beach and take shelter against the sea wall (why, is not clear) and on one occasion, sadly, they were machine-gunned and quite a lot of them were killed..... the north aisle may have been used on that occasion. Along with Keith Dimoline who lots of the older members of St Paul's will remember, Derek was a choir boy by then and recalls the boys being warned to keep out of the mortuary!

Terrifying times these must have been but the Cromwells also have happier memories of St Paul's. Liz had her 21st birthday party in the Whitecross Hall (and recalls that Derek's car tyres had been damaged when they left after the party!)

Stoker White is the elderly chap in the middle, but who can find Sheila Parkin?

Both of them remember 'Stoker' White, leader of the St Paul's scout pack... He was a bank cashier by profession, working at the bank at the corner of Clifton Road (and, according to Derek, counting the money very slowly and deliberately). Away from the formality of the bank, though, he always wore shorts, though a big chap. He drove around in a pre-war Austin tourer for years, marched the scouts and guides to church once a month and was obviously a much-loved eccentric character,(perhaps a bit like the larger-than-life characters in 'Dad's Army'!). He is spoken of fondly by quite a few people like Roger Walker who was in his scout pack, and Sheila Parkin (who even unearthed a photograph).

He seems to have been a kind and godly man who loved the church and left money to St Paul's when he died. His sister or cousin, (opinion is divided on this matter) was the Sunday School leader, in Whitecross Hall before the war and later in the choir vestry (church office).

Church was a much more formal place in those days and after the building had been restored and the pews installed, Liz tells of taking their children to church and one of them slipping under the pew in front when standing on a kneeler, and making a bang. This resulted in much disapproval from the congregation and even the vicar, Preb Harrison, stopped speaking and glared. This incident promoted a move to another church by the Cromwells, but they eventually came back – as many people have done after leaving the church for various reasons.

Now it must bring Derek and Liz much joy to see children and grandchildren (and a great grandchild!) in the St Paul's family!

The Cromwells, the Bishop and the Vicar on our 100th anniversary
Photo courtesy of Weston Mercury

Helen Vukotic's connections with St Paul's seem to be the earliest I could find from today's congregation. In fact members of her family were in the choir which sang at the consecration service in 1912!

"My family's connections with St Paul's go right back to the beginning, when my grandfather and uncle were in the choir. I was a bridesmaid at a wedding here at the age of six. The

church at that time was in much the same condition as it had been after the bombing. The ceremony was held in the Lady Chapel, as the roof of the nave had gone and the floor was still strewn with rubble."

Wow, and we grumble about a little bit of cold! Incidentally, I remember Mary Radcliffe telling me once that she and Richard were married in St Andrew's Chapel. Sadly, I was unable to ask her for more information.

Helen goes on to tell more about her memories.

"I was brought up as a Methodist and started attending Anglican services at University. Prebendary Harrison was vicar of St Paul's then, but was soon succeeded by Viv Payne. I lived and worked away from Weston for many years, but always came to St Paul's when visiting my parents, and Joan Tapley regarded my children as honorary members of the Sunday School.

My mother used to arrive well before the service began, armed with needle and thread and ready to darn any surplice that had developed a hole. (This, you younger ones, was before the days of built in obsolescence!) My father was a carpenter and when my mother died he gave to the church a flower stand that he had made from light oak (his favourite wood), in her memory. He outlived her by 31 years and is remembered by many older members of the congregation. I am proud to be following in the footsteps of my grandfather and parents and hope to continue to serve St Paul's for many years to come."

Helen certainly does 'serve St Paul's', - preparing the communion table, serving communion, helping to run the Mothers' Union, and on Tuesday afternoons working with those who need a bit of help with literacy and numeracy. She is also the Tradecraft rep.

Helen's father is lovingly remembered, especially by those who were children in the seventies and eighties. He knew the names and addresses of all the children in choir and Sunday School and sent each of them a birthday card, always with a coin attached with Sellotape. Certainly my children thought this was wonderful! He really was the children's friend!

Cecil collected stamps throughout the year, too, I remember, which he sent to the Children's Society – to raise money. He would come round to all of us at coffee time in the hall, at the end of the year armed with his little notebook. We each had to pay to guess how many stamps he'd collected during the year. The

Cecil Jeffery in his garden

winner got a small prize and the Children's Society got the money.

For years he also put up, decorated and took down the huge Christmas tree we had in church in those days and I remember when he was 'getting on a bit', my husband, Ian and Alan Brinkley being roped in to help. They had to follow his instructions to the letter and put all the decorations back in the box in just the right places. This caused great hilarity!

What a character. He was also a very keen gardener, often bringing his surplus produce to church to share, and he made his own wine. In fact, I think that the winner of the stamp competition got a bottle of his wine as a prize.

Joan Tapley sits quietly, these days, at the 9-30 service but over the years she has had great influence in our church, particularly as a result of her work with children and young people. She tells me she has been coming to the church for 75 years! Can anyone beat that? Joan came to St Paul's to the Sunday School and tells how much more formal things were in those days. She was taught by Miss White but to this day has no idea what her first name was.

Joan, like the Cromwells, remembers vividly the bombing of the church in 1941. She was a child then and couldn't believe that a thing like that could happen to a church. A church was supposed to be the safest of places. She was horrified and remembers the sheets of tarpaulin used to temporarily separate the south aisle from the nave. Everything was in a terrible mess and Joan was very upset by the damage to the main altar and the pulpit. As a child she liked to gaze at these things, thinking them very beautiful. Now they were horribly blackened but at least she was relieved to find they were still reasonably intact. And the spirit of St Paul's survived. Services still went on in St Andrew's Chapel and the south aisle.

Joan remembers spending time sometimes at the Good Shepherd as well as at St Paul's and says there was much toing and froing between the two churches. There was great sadness when the Good Shepherd closed.

When Joan had her own four children she used to walk them to church at St Paul's along with Mark Bowden, his sister and brother, and "Tony Windell who was accident prone". Viv Payne who was vicar by then after being based, earlier, as curate at the Good Shepherd, must have looked at Joan's 'walking bus' (there's nothing new under the sun!) and seen potential in this situation. Miss White had by now retired and there was no-one to run the Sunday School. What Viv Payne actually asked Joan was to run it for a couple of weeks until they found a permanent replacement for Miss White. She retired after running it for 30 years, ("officially 28 years, the first two were an apprenticeship"). Joan remembers very happy times at the Sunday School and recalls how much the older members of the congregation loved it when the children went into church to 'do' things at Christmas and Easter and Mothering Sunday.

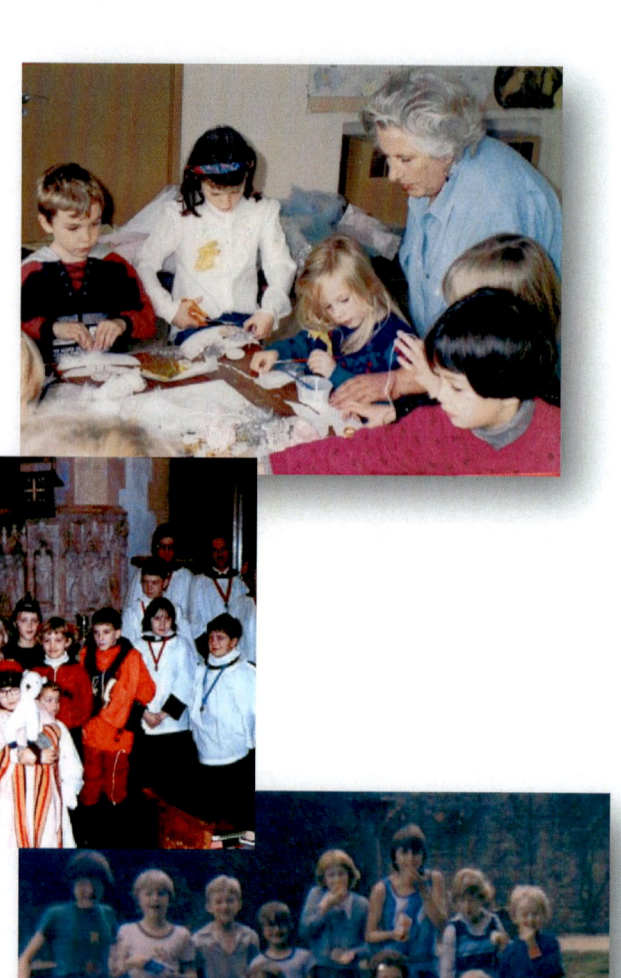

They always did something at Christmas. Once, all the children dressed up in costume singing carols and telling Christmas stories and legends from other countries and on another occasion Joan persuaded the vicar to let her bring a real donkey into church. He agreed on the understanding that she had to clear up any mess it made. It was exemplary, however, and stood quietly throughout the proceedings.

Running the Sunday School was not always easy. Some of the children who attended came from 'Tranquil House', a Muller Home for disturbed children, and they were anything but tranquil! Joan remembers the lady who ran the home, Margaret Williams, for whom the work was a labour of love and the atmosphere there was that of a loving home rather than an institution.

Joan also remembers – as lots of us do, the Kettle family – Dr Austin Kettle, his wife Mollie and their children. She remembers their kindness and support for her and her family throughout her husband's illness and during the years when she was singlehandedly bringing up her four lively and talented children.

As Joan's children grew, while still running the Sunday School, she began to help the Parkins run the youth club, or 'Go Club' as it was known. She also – having been introduced to Evelyn Christenson's book, 'What Happens when Women Pray' – was a prime mover in setting up women's prayer groups and a prayer chain here at St Paul's.

 Mark Boden, one of the members of Joan's 'walking bus' has now returned to St Paul's and comes on Tuesday afternoon to work with Helen Vukotic.

Mark remembers, "I started coming to Sunday School when I was 6 or 7 years old. Mrs Tapley, who lives near me, brought me with her own children. Mrs Tapley, Mrs Williams and Mrs Banwell were my teachers. When I was 14 I started serving in church. I did this for about 5 years.

When I was 11 or 12 I went to the youth club. It was run by Alan and Jane Brinkley. We used to play snooker and table tennis. I used to enjoy the Harvest supper. We had ham, a jacket potato and salad and a slice of gateau for pudding. After the meal we were entertained by the members of the church."

The 60's, 70's and 80's

Many of our older members will, I'm sure, remember life at St Paul's in these years, so forgive me if I get anything wrong.

St Paul's, like many churches, I think, was subject to cultural changes in the society of that time. People in general no longer automatically expected to spend their Sunday mornings at church. They questioned the faith that earlier generations had taken for granted. There were many influences bringing about changes in our society – too numerous to explore in any depth here, but churches everywhere were beginning to feel the effects. (I do remember Noel McKittrick blaming television in general and a serialisation of the 'Forsythe Saga' in particular for the demise of Evensong here at St Paul's.)

There were problems inside the church too during these years but the problems seemed to result in something happening that the bishop, in the consecration service in 1912, foretold when he warned that, *"The ordinary people of the church will have a much greater role to play in years to come."*

Already the people of St Paul's had lived through the devastation of two wars and the restoration of the building. They'd practised hospitality at the Whitecross Hall and the hall of the Good Shepherd and they'd had to work hard to raise money for the restoration. Now, there was what I can only call a 'flowering' of the social aspects of church life, involving many of the congregation in running the various activities. There grew up a strong Social Committee that organised all sorts of events. There was the Friendship Circle, the Revellers, The Go Club, there were church fetes, the Harvest Supper, barn dances, the Monday Whist evening and the memorable holidays organised by Peter Down.

All that was going on made St Paul's an attractive, vibrant, warm and welcoming place. It drew people in from outside and bound people together to counteract the effect of the problems. It prepared people for the kind of momentous changes that were just round the corner.

The 'Cleese' fete.

God surely knew what he was doing with us during those years and a strong, hospitable, capable community developed.

More Memories

Ann Cherry's memories start in the 40's but she remembers particularly the strong involvement of her parents, Frank and Irene Porter, in later years.

"Sue and I came to Sunday School at St Paul's in the late nineteen forties. The classes were held in the vestry and our teacher was called Miss White. She was a lovely lady who always looked the same, in a tweed coat and a brown felt hat

which had a ribbon band with a feather in it. She rode around the parish on a 'sit up and beg' bicycle.

The family moved to St Paul's Road in the late fifties and started attending St Paul's regularly. Father started the Planned Giving Scheme in the seventies. 'So much easier to balance the books when we know how much is coming in.'

Another cry of his was, "It doesn't run on hot water, you know!" He was very active in raising funds for the 'new' church hall, along with many others, and also ran an 'antiques auction' to raise money to equip the hall.

Mother was secretary of the PCC for years and edited the Parish Magazine. With Ethel Morgan she ran the Friendship Circle for 13 years. Ethel was Chairman and Mother, Secretary. Noel and the PCC presented them with leather bound ASBs for 13 years loyal service when they retired. This must have been in the late eighties as Noel was vicar from 1981 – 1992.

I was married at St Paul's in 1963 and my daughter, Judith, was christened at the 10.30 Family Service in September, 1967, one of the first babies to have a public baptism at St Paul's.

Mother was involved, with many others, in the Social Committee which catered for all sorts of functions in the church during Vivian's and Noel's time."

Irene Porter and the Kettles

What hard workers the Porters were and they were such kind, pleasant people. They always chatted to our children and took an interest in what they were doing at school. I always think of them in conjunction with the Frank and Ethel Morgan with whom they were great friends. Ethel Morgan and Irene Porter, as Ann mentions, ran the wonderful St Paul's 'Friendship Circle' for many years. It was a lively and friendly club for the older church people and I remember that each member received a card on their birthday. Looking through an old church magazine for February, 1982, supplied by John Davies, I was interested to read in a short report about the previous month's meeting of the Friendship Circle, that, *"Over 100 members and guests spent a very happy, friendly afternoon in the Parish Hall – the entertainment was supplied by our own members and was thoroughly enjoyed by all."*

I remember, in connection with the Friendship Circle being invited to the Christmas tea and entertainment. The tables had been cleared and we sat back in anticipation. Suddenly a lady stood up and said she wanted to sing. We clapped politely and off she went. The trouble was that she couldn't sing in tune but there was simply no stopping her. Mrs Cleese, who was sitting in front of me rummaged through her handbag, took out a large handkerchief and stuffed it into her mouth to stop herself laughing out loud. (I half expected the incident to feature in an episode of Monty Python!)

I remember vividly too when people from the St Paul's Revellers staged 'This is Your Life' for Frank Porter. He really entered into the spirit of the thing and the show caused much hilarity. And now Ann carries on the hospitable traditions of her parents by making delicious cakes and sandwiches, and helping to run St Paul's Seniors.

Pam Burnell's parents, Audrey and Cyril Savill, like the Porters were active members of the church from the early seventies until 1986.

"Dad was Treasurer for many years and he and John Davies and Bill Green all assisted each other. He was also a regular member of the choir and used to take part in the Harvest Supper activities.

Mum organised the flowers for many years and Gloria Davies was a member of her team of helpers. She was also an active member of the monthly Friendship Circle which was held in the Hall and was very popular. I had a clothes and wool shop in Whitecross Road in the 1980's and on one occasion I organised a Fashion Show for the Friendship Circle, using members as models!

My daughter, Sarah, attended confirmation classes in Rev Vivian Payne's time and was confirmed in 1980."

And now Pam, like Ann, follows in the family tradition as a flower arranger and is very involved in the pastoral team at the church.

Ken and Sheila Parkin and their children, **Liz and Nigel**, arrived at St Paul's in the early sixties. They came from Devon originally (where Sheila had spent the war years making parts for Spitfires!) but Ken was now teaching in Nailsea and eventually in Weston. They soon became very involved in life at St Paul's where under the leadership of John and Ada Neville there was much interest in the CMS movement, and the church PCC sponsored young people to go on holidays run by CMS each August.

After the first of these holidays, in Jersey, in 1974, Ken and Sheila, with Mary and Richard Radcliffe started a youth club, known as the 'Go Club' (Go into all the world and preach the Gospel). Liz, Sheila's daughter, listed other adventurous holidays the Go Club members attended. These included

Egypt in 1975, the Norfolk Broads in '77 and 'Mayflower', London (The headquarters of CMS) in '76

Liz remembers they did community work in the parish, such as gardening for the elderly, singing at Christmas in nursing homes and they fundraised for CMS.

Members of the Go Club, going….

JERSEY SAFARI CAMP
St. Ouen's Bay, Channel Islands
August 16-26
Overseas to this island in the sun. Glorious sandy beaches, surf-riding, swimming expeditions. A camp under canvas within the sound of the sea, with opportunities for service and for discovering the excitement of real Christianity.
Cost: £22*
    (This covers meals and accommodation)**
Age: 13-16
Leaders:
    Mr Ron Parkinson
    Mr and Mrs Jim Stanley-Smith
Applications to:
    Mr Ron Parkinson, 21 Fairsnape Road, Lytham, Lytham St. Annes, Lancs FY8 4HG

.... to Jersey

Lesley Money also kindly supplied her memories of the Go Club.

"We met on Sunday evenings and played games etc. There were always lots of young people

there. It was good making friends with others from the church.

Go Club was part of CMS so we got involved in different CMS projects and fund-raising activities. This included wheeling a pram of bricks round Bristol! (I think we were raising money for the Sudan). We learned new songs which were quite different from the traditional hymns we sang in church. The vicar's wife, Dorothy Payne played the guitar along with some of the Go Club members. Sometimes we were allowed to sing our songs in church, accompanied by those guitars. I am not sure that all the congregation appreciated the 'new' songs."

Like Liz, Lesley remembers the holidays and that, "We had to write an account of the holiday and then present it at an evening afterwards." She goes on to say, "These holidays were camps where we met other young people from church youth groups from different parts of the country. We had fun together as well as interesting and enlightening Bible studies, and amazing worship. Each camp had a resident CMS mission partner who worked with us and told us about their work in different countries. I found them very inspiring people. I learnt so much from being with other Christians from a range of backgrounds. I thoroughly enjoyed these annual holidays."

As well as running the youth club Ken and Sheila were hall caretakers for a while, helped to run the Sunday School in

Miss White's time, started the St Paul's involvement in the Wessex Walks (and Sheila completed the whole walk, from Weston to Wells several times!). They were members of the 'Revellers' and Ken, with Peter Down, also ran the Monday night whist evening in the hall for 29 years. Another busy family! They left St Paul's for a while when they went to live at Lympsham but came back and were pleased to find St Paul's just as warm and welcoming.

John and Ada Neville came to St Paul's at Easter, 1961. Ada had been a nurse and John was a solicitor and had come to work in a Weston firm. Both had a deep faith and a strong commitment to the work of CMS. John wanted to be a Reader and approached the vicar, Preb Harrison, on this subject but was told, *"I don't want a Reader, I want a Churchwarden."* So, for several years John served as Churchwarden and remembers, in the terrible winter of 1962/3, walking to church through the thick snow at 6-00am to make sure the boiler was on to warm the church.

John did become a Reader and remained so until 1973 when, after studying for 3 years at Salisbury, he was ordained and became a non-stipendiary minister along with Dr Michael Hinton who had been Headmaster of Broadoak School. (Michael subsequently left to take up work in Dover, eventually publishing "The Hundred Minute Bible" which, according to Bishop Pritchard in its preface, is for people who, *"want an easy access into the Christian story"*, and *"for Christians who want to revisit the big picture."*)

So, John became Rev John Neville and he and Ada continued to support the work of CMS, even to the extent, much later, of requesting donations for CMS instead of presents on the

> 16th November 2000
>
> Dear Mr and Mrs Neville
>
> Thank you very much for your generous donation of £1330:00 for the Under Tree Schools project in Sudan. This will be sent via the Rev. Joseph Ayok to be used in Sudan. Please pass on our most sincere thanks to those who contributed to your Golden Wedding Anniversary Celebrations.
>
> The most recent news we have on this project was from Mr Richard Steuart who supervised the teacher training and opening of Under Tree Schools. Thirteen selected Sudanese men attended this training. Some had previous experience of teaching, two had been headmasters, others had minimal teaching experience and some had none at all.
>
> The training focused primarily on teaching principles and techniques. During the second week each teacher presented a class and was critiqued by his fellow classmates and by Richard. He reported that the students were attentive and enthusiastic throughout the lessons, attendance was good and that each day began with a student reading a Bible passage.
>
> On completion of the teacher training the teachers guides and school supplies were divided among the schools represented. Richard stayed on in Sudan to visit the schools during the first five weeks of term to monitor the progress in establishing schools and the quality of teaching. He concluded his report by saying "the teachers are to be complemented on their perseverance and generally positive attitude. This was evidenced in the start up of the schools and the continued operation of these schools". CMS is delighted to be involved with this project in southern Sudan.
>
> Thank you again for your interest and support.
>
> Tristan Heath - Fund-raising Department

occasion of their Golden Wedding.

John has worked hard and tirelessly for the people of St Paul's and has been a devoted and faithful visitor of the housebound and of those in hospital... He could often be seen until recently, in his robes, striding along to take communion especially to those living in the many residential/ nursing homes in the parish. He has also, for several years arranged the Christmas carol service at Clarence House where he now lives (and which, until Viv Payne's time was the St Paul's Vicarage).

John remembers with pleasure the many social activities at the church and an appearance he made in one of the Revellers' productions when he was King Canute... He remembers 'Stoker' White regularly bringing the scouts to church and a special stand being made for their flags. And he remembers with great pleasure the interregnum between Noel McKittrick and Huw Davies, - as one of the happiest times of his life, when for that year he was priest in charge.

We members of the congregation at that time noticed and commented on how relaxed and confident John became during that year. It was a pleasure to see how well he filled the role. During that time, John started a group to pray regularly for God's guidance in the choice of the new vicar and these prayers resulted in Huw Davies coming to St Paul's. Since then John has continued his work and although no longer very mobile he still offers ministry to anyone who has need of it during the 9. 30 a.m. Communion.

Cymru am byth

I don't know whether it was the result of having a Welsh vicar or simply the fact that Wales is only just over the water from Weston, but quite a few of the families at St Paul's in the 60's came from Wales – although I only know of one person, Rita Mitchell, who is a Welsh speaker (though Dave in our present choir seems to have a smattering!)

Joyce and Gerry Williams came from Wales to St Paul's in 1957 when Gerry took up a teaching post at what was then Uphill School (on the site of the present 'University Campus' of Weston College). Later on both Joyce and Gerry taught at Uphill Primary School. Coming from strongly Christian families they looked for a church that would suit them and found St Paul's to be warm and welcoming (and with a vicar whose voice was decidedly hoarse after an international match at Cardiff!). Joyce, like many others remembers Miss White, an elderly lady by now, *who "took the few children we had into the vestry for Sunday School. The children then mostly came from Tranquil House, a children's home run by a very capable lady called Margaret Williams. The children,"* as we have already heard from Joan Tapley, *"were anything but tranquil and led Miss Williams a merry dance!"*

Other memories of Viv Payne's time involve regular parish outings after the morning service and Joyce tells of one occasion when, *"we travelled by car to the Quantocks and had a picnic at Greatwood after a walk. Then we had evensong in the open air. Dorothy Payne played her guitar and we sang some choruses. We also played cricket and rounders and sang 'All Things Bright and Beautiful'. On the way home we stopped for a drink in a country pub. A lovely evening."*

Joyce also recalls, "We appeared on TV twice, once for 'Songs of Praise and a second time for the televising of a family service which was an innovation for those days. We had to sit right at the front because our children were very young at the time, Kathy, the youngest, being only three years old. That was in 1968. Our son, Gareth was head choir boy then. He couldn't sing but Viv Payne insisted that all the young people should take part in church life. The choirmaster told Gareth to mime. That experience put him off church for life!"

Another of Joyce's memories involves a coach trip run by the Social Committee much later on.

(I remember that nightmare occasion very vividly, as I was Secretary of the Social Committee at the time and responsible for arranging the trip that went horribly wrong!) Joyce says of that evening, *"We went on an evening coach trip, a mystery tour, which went on and on. We were the young ones then and had to do a day's work before setting off. Anyway, we thought we would never reach our destination. Eventually, starving hungry, we reached the pub where we were going to eat."* (The 'Tom Mogg', it was called. The name is engraved on my memory for all time.) Joyce continues, *"Being young and polite we waited for the older members of the party to help themselves to food first, only to find, when it was our turn, that all the food had disappeared onto their piled- high plates. A second amount was brought out but by this time the older ones were ready for their second helpings."* Oh dear, what a disaster, and the Brinkleys had brought along a young French student who was staying with them. Goodness knows what she thought.

Songs of Praise

John and Gloria Davies who eventually brought up their family in Uphill, like the Williamses, moved to Clifton Road in 1961 when the vicar was Preb Harrison. John recalls *"When Preb Harrison died and Viv Payne was appointed, he requested that a new modern vicarage be built next to the old one which became Clarence House. A few years later the money from the sale of the Whitecross Hall went towards the building of a new church hall on the same site of the church."* John goes on to talk about the changes Viv Payne made in the services. *"In the early days"*, he says, *"Viv Payne introduced a short, 9.30 service followed by the traditional, well attended 11am service of matins. There was also an 8am Communion and Evensong. Viv subsequently combined the two morning services into one 11am Holy Communion service. There was a large, full choir of boys and men and once a month St Paul's Scouts under the leadership of 'Stoker' White used to parade to church."*

John recalls, *"Planned giving was introduced into the diocese, and to St Paul's by Frank Porter, in the seventies. A team of people visited the parishioners to see if they would sign an undertaking to give a set amount for three years. The team would revisit at the end of that time. Subsequently the scheme has been developed to include a gift-aid declaration and the other main change in giving is that while many give by weekly envelope, there are now many who pay by standing order...a sign of the times."*

John and Gloria have, over the years, played a large part in organising the distribution of envelopes and John, along with Tony Jeffery, (who also has Welsh connections) can still be found almost every Sunday morning, after the 9-30 service, counting the collection.

Other memories John has are of a *"Flourishing youth club"* and some members, he says went on visits to Taize. He tells too that a *"German Boys' Choir used to visit St Paul's. They were housed by parishioners and always gave a concert."*

John and Gloria, and Joyce and Gerry and Tony Jeffery have all served as churchwardens as well as fulfilling all sorts of other roles. Gloria was, I think, Secretary of the Social Committee for some time and ran the flower team for several years. Joyce helped Joan to run the Sunday School and she and Gerry were members of the Revellers as well as running house groups and helping with Alpha courses. Both couples were, I think, founder members of the Uphill Bible study group started by Michael Hinton (and it's still going!)

While looking through old St Paul's magazines I was reminded of a rather tragic event affecting both families when, on Sunday, 13 December, 1981 the sea surged through Uphill and both their houses were flooded. In the churchwardens' report for the year John and Gerry refer to that night and to the help they received from their church friends.

"At the end of a year of varying anxieties, the Uphill flood, which entered the homes of both church wardens was a blow. We all very much appreciated your sincerely expressed messages of sympathy and many kind acts and offers of help, which included cleaning, meals, accommodation, Christmas fare and baths."

Whilst on the subject of churchwardens, I'm sure, many people still remember the unforgettable **Agnes Sands,** who I think was the first lady churchwarden, serving with my husband, Ian, on his first stint as warden. She had worked as a nurse in a London hospital and at the beginning of the war her father begged her to go home to Kent where they lived. He said London was going to be too dangerous. She dutifully returned as requested but spent the rest of the war working in a field hospital in Dover and praying every night, *"Dear Lord, please don't let them bomb the generators tonight, we need them, to operate."*

Before retiring to live in Weston, Agnes had later been Matron of a hospital in Wells and had all the organisational skills that we associate with the redoubtable ladies that once fulfilled that role. She was also kind and supportive to anyone who needed help. I particularly remember her persuading me that I could become a flower arranger and without my knowing about it she took a photograph of my first humble effort and arranged for me to watch Phyllis Rowlett and learn from her. I know that Ian developed a great affection for Agnes, as I think did anyone with whom she came into contact. She also had a wicked sense of humour.

The Good Shepherd

What was life like at the Good Shepherd Church?

Hilary Hughes has lots of happy memories of the church during the 1950's and 60's

"The church always had a curate from St Paul's but he was always in charge at the Good Shepherd. I can remember Rev Thursfield in the 50's and in the 60's, Vivian Payne (who went to be Vicar of Bedminster and returned to St Paul's as vicar), Rev Meredith and Rev Kerslake.

It was a tin church but inside it was beautifully appointed with plain windows and walls panelled in wood. The pulpit, lectern, alter-rails and fronts of the choir stalls were also made of wood, a lot of it beautifully carved by Strode Pitman, my great uncle. He worshipped at the church and was churchwarden there for many years and lived in Whitting Road. There were dark blue velvet curtains over the doors and alter, pulpit and lectern 'falls' all changed for the different seasons and carefully looked after with any mending done by the 'Sewing Party'. The Good Shepherd also had a proper pipe organ, played for many years by a Mr Dyer who had been Headmaster at Uphill School.

On the right of the doorway, as you entered the church through a porch, was a beautiful Children's Corner. It contained a small cross, books, wooden font (now at St Paul's) and little vases of fresh flowers on what was like a mini altar. It was always beautifully kept, though the children used it a lot. On the left were three rows of choir stalls and I remember them always being full but just of men.

Worship on Sunday consisted of an 8am Communion, 11am Matins and 6.30 Evensong. I think there was a midweek communion too and Sunday School was at 2.30pm in the church and hall (a tin hall behind the church with a very pokey kitchen, toilets and cloakroom). Gift days were held regularly each year to keep the church 'up together' and provide money for missions. It was a financially viable church with money in hand even when it closed. Dad was Treasurer for years, which is how I know.

There were lots of activities in the hall. Sunday School was held there, Harvest Supper, with 100 seated and entertainment on the good-sized stage. There was a youth club, the Sewing Party and their sales of work, jumble sales, men's group, whist drives etc and the hall was let out for various activities – the Brownies was one. I particularly remember the Harvest Suppers which were great occasions with all the tickets sold out. It was all prepared and washing up done in the tiny kitchen and we had ham, tongue, salad and trifles. Mrs Carter was the caretaker of the hall. She was a tiny, round Welsh lady and played the piano. Despite her size, one had to beware of her as she was fierce and had to be humoured. Woe betide anyone who left any mess behind after a jumble sale!

The church was always full. It served the Devonshire Road area up as far as Windwhistle Road and included all the side roads. Lots of families came. We had coach outings in summer and one sticks in my memory when we had a lovely picnic by a stream. The church always had a link with the Church Army and I loved it when Sister Brookfield came and spoke at Matins and at special children's services. She was very round and always had lovely stories illustrated with pictures and other items. The Good Shepherd was a very happy place. As a child I loved to be there and the grown-ups were always kind and loving, part of my family. In fact, the Good Shepherd was a family." (No wonder there was such sadness when it was closed.)

Hilary , though she did marry Alex Hughes who came all the way from Cheddar, grew up in this area.

While gathering information for this book, however, it has become clear to me that many of the St Paul's congregation have come here from somewhere else and perhaps that is one reason for the lack of the kind of cliques that sometimes develop in some churches and make life difficult for any newcomers. St Paul's loves newcomers, welcomes them in and finds them a job to do!

Many people at St Pauls will have got to know **Kenn and Ena King** professionally over the years in their capacity as Driving Instructors...and they too came here 'from somewhere else' as Ena remembers:

"It was in 1966 that we first came to live in Weston-super-Mare, from Tobruk in Libya. We lived in a spacious flat in Clevedon Road just up from the sea and Pool and opposite a lovely lady, Mrs Robins, who introduced us to St Paul's Church. The Rev Payne was the vicar then. The children, on Sundays were taken into the choir vestry (now the office) by Miss White and instructed in the Bible stories.

Kenn, my husband, came with us on alternate Sundays. He was stationed at Northolt near Heathrow, in the RAF, but housing was better here than in the rabbit warrens they offered us up there, so for the next 3 years he used the excellent train service to London that we still have. Having a sister living in Winscombe helped me.

Our two girls, Sarah and Alison, joined the Brownies at the Good Shepherd 'tin' Church belonging to St Paul's and sometimes attended the main church with the cubs and scout groups parading up the road. Later they both joined the St Paul's choir and stayed with it until they left college many years later.

Kenn, Sarah and Alison were all confirmed at the same time by the Bishop and we all celebrated in our new hall. The new hall, when it was built, was a grand affair and played a large part in our lives, building up friendships between young and old. It was used for Harvest Suppers, visiting bishops, the Revellers and their entertainments – for pantos and shows, with a lovely stage and the boiler room for a dressing room. It brought everyone together.

The St Paul's magazine was a lively affair and I have enclosed an entry about 'my girls', aged 18 and 20 at the time. Ten years later, Alison got married here on a lovely but blustery day. That will be 25 years ago on January 2nd, 2013.

The King Family

News from 'Our Kings'
Sarah writes from Hong Kong –
'Here is a little more information of what I do other than my work. Sport is the main event out here. I took part in the W.R.A.C.'s Dragon Boat Race in June, we came third in our heat, but did not make the finals. It took a lot of our time practising for the event, but was great fun. I am a member of the H.Q.B.F. (Headquarters British Forces) H.M.S. Tamar Volley Ball team and play regularly against teams all over Hong Kong (like inter-County Sports) and joint Services teams, excluding the Royal Hong Kong Police force. I represent my troop in the Inter-Troop Volley Ball Championships against teams from Ghurka units in Hong Kong/Kowloon only. Our troop won in July and I was one of only two W.R.A.C. players to take part. I also swim for the troop, being the only girl to swim in the Inter-troop Gala. We have the British Forces Championships in Sek Kong this month. This includes all of Hong Kong, Kowloon and the New Territories. I shall be in it with 7 other girls from Army and Navy Units. My best wishes to all my friends at St. Paul's – I often think of you all – Sarah King'.

Congratulations to Alison
Alison begins her new job on Tuesday, 18th August, as nanny to Rupert 6 and Victoria 4. These are the children of the International Show-jumping and Eventing husband and wife team – Gail and Toby Sturgis. Alison is to live as part of the family on the 200 acre farm in Great Somerford, Wiltshire, and to go riding and hunting. Victoria's best friend is Master Peter Phillips, who lives 4 miles away, so Alison is expecting to see quite a lot of the Queen's grandson.

St. Paul's Magazine, September 1981

St Paul's has been the centre of our lives in this area, even when we downsized from our house to a bungalow in Hutton village, four miles away. It was still St Paul's we came to because our friends are here. Changes, brought about by different vicars have been noticeable and serving on the PCC in Huw's time was challenging. Starting up the office with Ian Todd was a very good move.

Andrew has carried on Huw's innovations and has done well with many more people coming in for friendship. He made things so easy for me at Kenn's funeral. I now attend not only the early service but sometimes the one at 11am and the Seniors' tea every fourth Friday, as well as some extra events. So it is still the main part of my life and I am honoured to still be a reader there."

Bill and Liz Green certainly did come from 'somewhere else', both growing up in service families. Bill was born in India, in Rawalpindi and Liz in Egypt. They met in Kenya where they were both working, and married and both their children were born in Kenya. (All this seems very Romantic to someone who grew up in a mining village in South Yorkshire!). When they returned to England, they lived in Worle for a time but moved to Weston and to St Paul's, in 1976. Bill ran a Post Office in town and Liz taught at Weston College. Liz has a great love of music and was soon a member of the choir here (as ladies were now accepted!), and she has shared some memories which also sparked off a few of mine.

"During the interregnum following Rev Payne's retirement in the mid-nineteen seventies the choir filled the choir stalls and included soprano, alto, tenor, bass and children's voices.

When Rev Noel McKittrick was appointed Vicar, his wife, Christa (a very accomplished organist/pianist) eventually took on the position of organist and choir mistress. During this time the choir, (augmented by anyone who was interested and enthusiastic) rehearsed and presented several Roger Jones musicals at St Paul's. We also joined with other choirs from around the area to perform the musicals at other churches, Weston Playhouse and even at the Colston Hall in Bristol." It was all very exciting.

"*Christa also encouraged junior members of the choir to form a small instrumental group to accompany the choir and two of the young choristers became excellent organists. Music played a very important part in the services and in the life of the church.*

On Rev McKittrick's retirement, Philip Goode took over as choirmaster. He was a keen supporter of the Royal School of Church Music and during his time here, members of the choir attended many training days." (Memorable ones were courses with Margaret Rizza and John Bell at Taunton and one occasion when some of us, along with people from other churches, rehearsed and sang Stainer's magnificent 'Crucifixion'.)

"Philip also encouraged the choir for quite a few years to take part in the annual Choral Festival at Wells" (and I will never forget processing into the cathedral through the great west door, being part of the thrilling sound of a few hundred voices singing in unison in that beautiful building, and joining in a magnificent act of worship. On one occasion the Bishop - I think it was Jim Thompson - said it sounded like angels singing. We loved it, although it was hard work, and we loved being rehearsed and conducted for several years by the wonderfully talented Malcolm Archer who was not only a marvellous arranger of music but could also sing **all** the parts himself!)

Liz remembers too we also took part in a recording of Songs of Praise at Exeter Cathedral.

She goes on to say, *"Following the appointment of Huw Davies as Vicar, the morning communion service was brought forward to 9.30 and a second service started at 11.00, mainly for young families and with a worship group providing the* music. With no young people joining as choristers the choir now only numbers about eleven adults. Philip has retired and Iris Lyndon is organist/ choir mistress."

As Liz mentioned, Christa encouraged young people in the choir and three of those youngsters, **Victoria, Kerry and Oliver Johnson** really deserve a special mention for the contribution they made to life at St Paul's. They came to church on their own and I think they may have come to Sunday School to start with but they soon joined the choir and the instrumental group. Victoria, with Christa's encouragement, became a very competent organist, read bio-chemistry at university and then worked in cancer research. A few years later, however, Victoria, after a further course of study, was ordained and is now a vicar in Manchester.

Kerry was the artistic member of the family (and designed the very modern cover for St Paul's Church magazine in Huw's time). She came back to St Paul's for her wedding and the choir members were thrilled to sing for her. Oliver was a showman and enjoyed taking part in the Revellers' shows, as did his sisters. They were very talented young people and we were all very fond of them.

The other organ student taught by Christa was Martin Lee who also became a vicar and now lives and works in Durham.

Liz not only sings in the choir but has also, for years, run the Mothers' Union with stalwart help from Helen Vukotic, Val

Robinson and Gaye Carter and she has memories to tell of that.

"An old MU banner, displayed to the right of the altar is evidence of an early branch at St Paul's. However this had ceased to function at some stage. When Noel McKittrick became Vicar in the mid nineteen seventies his wife, Christa, restarted the branch which continues to this day. Membership varies between 20 and 35, and members currently come from 5 local churches. Meetings are held on a Monday morning, when there may be a speaker or another activity. Mothers' Union is concerned with family life and Christa, with the help of the St Paul's branch, started a Mother and Toddler Group. At first it was every other week but by February, 1988, it had become a weekly event on a Wednesday morning, and this still continues. From its beginnings when it catered for a small number of mainly church families it has grown into an outreach project to the whole town and the number of children attending on a recent Wednesday morning was 68! The group is now called 'SPARKS' (St Paul's Active And Ready Kids), and is run in the church by the curate's wife, Mims Yacomeni, with help from members of the congregation, the original Mothers' Union members having, at last, retired."

Toddler outing. Who do you recognise?
Mothers' Union catering.

Olive Money has lots of memories to share with us from her days on the Social Committee, time spent as Hall Secretary and writer/producer of many of the Revellers' shows. Her first memory, though, is of a Marriage Reunion she helped arrange during Noel McKittrick's time

"From time to time, we were urged to go out on 'Mission' and it was decided to have a Marriage Reunion in 1984 – welcoming all those who had been married at St Paul's. Sheila Parkin helped me to go through the church records and we made a list. The writing in these books was terrible and it was difficult to decipher the relevant details – but we did our best. There followed weeks of detective work, trying to track down the couples at their 1984 addresses. Initially I started calling on people, but that was a slow method. Then, the Vicar, Noel McKittrick, phoned me to say he'd 'booked' the Bishop for a date in June, but I had, at that point, only contacted 8 couples, so I decided I would have to speed things up by using the 'phone! This provided many amusing results. It was often a case of making an educated guess as to the identity of the person I was phoning. Several times when I thought I was ringing the wife, I discovered they had divorced and she was on her second marriage! Another time, as I worked my way down the list, I found I was ringing a father for the third time – he had omitted to tell me he had 3 daughters!

In the end we finished up with a list of 300 couples to be invited. Many were out of the area but many were living in the newly-developed area of Worle. So it was that John and I spent the whole of one Saturday, on our bikes, delivering these invitations by hand. Because some areas were new, we

couldn't find the roads and tradespeople were unable to help us.

Two days before the reunion, John had a heart attack and spent time in the Intensive Care Unit – so he missed the Reunion.

The oldest couple we found were traced to Burnham-on-Sea and the Vicar visited them but they were not well enough to come to the actual service. Richard and Mary Radcliffe were, we found, married in the side aisle of the ruined church after it was bombed (in 1941) – and they, in fact, cut the 'Wedding Cake' at the reception following the Reunion Service. "

Olive's second 'memory' is concerned with the famous Harvest Suppers and Revellers shows that so many people loved (performers and audiences).

"My husband's job brought the Money family from London to Weston in April, 1972. Our involvement with Guides and Air Cadets helped us to make friends and St Paul's Church made us feel very welcome. It was not long before I found myself involved with the Social Committee – which was really, at that time, a group of ladies who provided refreshments when asked. In September, 1973 we were expected to organise the Harvest Supper and it was while we were washing up that I discovered the entertainers were being paid to come. We ladies thought we would like to harness 'homegrown' talent for the following year – and so the 'Revellers' were born.

Some of the ladies on the committee persuaded husbands and families to join in and we put together a programme. The Vicar's wife, Dorothy, played the guitar and so did another adult and two of the children but we needed a pianist and Hilda Goold persuaded her husband, Vernon, to fill the role. Some people may remember Vernon Goold – he was, at one time, Mayor. He was a proficient pianist but had to be "kept in order" – so his wife sat beside him to perform that job. His party piece was 'Land of Hope and Glory' which he always wanted to play at rehearsals.

The programme for that first show was quite simple. Staging it on the small platform in the hall, though, was a major problem. There were about 15 of us on the stage. We had to have very basic costumes – the ladies wore blouses and long skirts, then we could add hats and shawls for the finish (songs from Old Time Music Halls with the audience joining in). The men wore simple shirts and trousers, adding caps and waistcoats for the finale. We had to make our entrances out of the boiler room and we managed to conceal our entrances - and the piano, behind screens which were kindly donated............. We very much enjoyed our rehearsals and the audience was very appreciative.

The custom at St Paul's then was to provide a social occasion in February before Lent began – sometimes it was simply a 'Candlelight Supper' but for 1975 the Revellers felt encouraged to perform a 'potted panto' and we chose to do 'Ali Baba' – there should have been 40 thieves but we could only muster seven! The script was very loosely based on the original story. Vernon Goold, our former pianist, wanted to take part and he became 'Ally Oop' with a market stall selling bric-a-brac and saucy seaside postcards. He was so determined to look right for the part that he went to Weston College to be rigged out and called at my house, one evening when I was in the house alone to see if I approved! He had on dark make-up and I didn't recognise him. He frightened me to death! I thought he was selling carpets!

To defeat the robbers we had 'tiger hunters' (bearing a strong resemblance to 'Dad's Army'). The ensuing battle was supposed to be with fake swords but Billy Blewett (an old gent who used to live nearby) insisted on bringing a real one – which nearly drew blood! Although we wouldn't have won any Oscars, everyone loved seeing normally sober-suited men dressing up and making fools of themselves.

The shows got more ambitious and ingenious. In 1978 we did one called 'Alice in the Waxworks' and took a look at English history and great ingenuity was shown in producing 'authentic' costumes. We started in total darkness and when the lights went up, we were in a Waxworks with a tableau of important characters in our history, singing new words to the 'Ascot Gavotte' from 'My Fair Lady'. Alice lingers too long and when the waxworks closes she sees all the characters come to life. At one point we had King Canute (John Neville) on Weston Prom, trying to rule the waves while monks in the background were frantically digging out the rhynes which *drained Sedgemoor. The show also had a scene where Henry the Eighth plays musical chairs with his wives and every time the music stopped one of the wives had to leave the stage. We had Mike Tedstone as Harold (with a rubber-tipped arrow stuck to his glasses), Ian Jerram as Cromwell and many others, including a gang of suffragettes.*

We did another panto, Cinderella, in 1979 and to cope with difficult technical problems we had two Fairy Godmothers (Ethel Morgan and Ena King) who constantly made a mess of their spells. The two ugly sisters were two local solicitors – and the audience really enjoyed their efforts. We thought the panto might be the last of our shows. The Vicar left, though, and Frank Morgan, a retired clergyman who coped with the interregnum asked us to entertain at the Harvest Supper."

And so began a long run of Harvest Supper entertainments.

"Throughout the existence of the 'Revellers' we were always welcoming new people and so our shows continued and we tried various different themes. In 1983 we 'visited' various countries. We went to a fashion show in Paris, we visited the Zuyder Zee , three men dressed in Japanese kimonos sang '3 Little Maids', and we even had two Italian icecream sellers singing 'Just One Cornetto'. 1984 had a Village Festival theme and the men made an excellent job of Morris Dancing, with scarves! In 1985 'All at Sea' was loosely based on Treasure Island with Long John Copper played by a

policeman. In 1987 we had great fun with 'The Clarence Park Holiday Camp'.

In 1988 I retired from producing shows and passed the responsibility on to Alan Brinkley – although I still took part."

All the social activites of those days may seem somewhat frivolous but as Olive suggested to me they did perhaps in some ways,' help to heal the hurt' caused by the closure of the Good Shepherd Church. I think they also forged ties of friendship between people which still exist today, and they created a strong, welcoming community, and a realisation of the importance of hospitality, (and fun!) in the life of the church.

The Waxworks Show

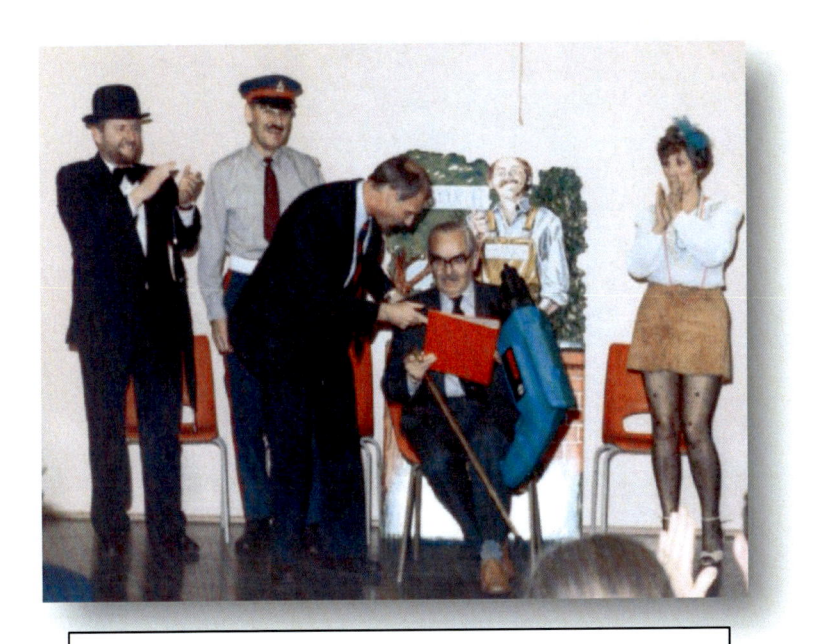

Above: Frank Porter, This is Your Life.
Below: Henry and his Wives, from 'Tudor Television'.

Above: Morris Dancers from 'On the Village Green'.
Below: Long John Copper and the Crew, from 'All at Sea'.

Above: Cheer Leaders from 'Guides and Dolls'.
Below: Nuns, wondering what to do about Maria.

Rites of passage.... growing up at St Paul's

"I feel very privileged to have grown up as part of the St Paul's Church family. My parents, Ian and Betty Jerram, started attending St Paul's regularly when I was about eight years old. I have very happy memories of both Church and Sunday School that I attended with my younger sister Esther. It was lead by Joan Tapley and Joyce Williams. My brother Simeon joined the Choir at a fairly early age, partly because he had an angelic voice and partly, I am sure, because in those days the child choristers were paid!

There was always lots going on socially, which helped to keep us all out of trouble during our teenage years, from Alan Brinkley's Youth Club to the Harvest Supper entertainments led by Olive Money and later Alan Brinkley. Olive was well known for planning everything meticulously down to where each person should be standing at any one time (worked out with the assistance of her pepper pots) and avoiding "the wrath of Olive" was a very strong incentive to learn our words. I still now know off by heart the words to many songs from music hall and the shows. Alan rebranded the shows a little and comedy became more of a feature.

Alan also took over from Ken Parkin and organised the annual Wessex Walk in aid of Save the Children, which our family regularly participated in. When I came back to Weston after my student years, my husband, Ian, joined us for a few years, until our children arrived. I was then promoted to "driver", dropping off and picking up Mum and Dad, whilst Ian took on post walk catering – Sunday dinner!

I also remember barn dances in the Church Hall and Youth Club social evenings including a curry evening which for some reason my Grandad attended. He claimed that it was the first time he had ever eaten curry which became something of a family joke because although he was known not to be adventurous with food, he did have a habit of adding curry powder to the most unlikely dishes as " seasoning".

My husband and I were married at St Paul's and a very joyous occasion it was too, with the Church full not only of our family and friends but also members of the congregation, many of whom had known me since I had started attending St Paul's. A few years after our wedding we had another family celebration at St Paul's for the joint Christening of our son, Jacob, and my sister's son, Sam, on Advent Sunday, which seemed very appropriate.

Sadly my father died last year and our last family celebration at the church was of his life. It seemed fitting for us to say goodbye to him in a place which had been such an important part of his life, which he had held in such affection and where my mother has found such love and support since his death.

What I miss most about being unable to attend Church regularly partly due to the children's weekend activities (primarily rugby!) is the rhythm of the Church year, something which I used to find a great support spiritually.

However when I am able to attend I still feel very welcome. I have very much appreciated the Church's outreach to Uphill Primary School which has enabled both my children to attend "Sunday School" as an after school club during the week, and also the opportunities at St Paul's for Worship and Fellowship for teenagers.

Society now is very different from when I was growing up and St Paul's has really moved with the times whilst still supporting those of us who remain more traditional in our spiritual needs. The celebrations for St Paul's 100th Birthday showed how much the Church has grown and adapted to the needs of the local community. It is still a warm and welcoming place to me for Worship as it was when I was growing up, but it now offers so much more, particularly to those who may not have had the same comfortable start in life as I did." **(Rebecca Parkman)**

All Change at St. Paul's

Alan and Jane Brinkley are very much involved in life at St Paul's today and Alan has lots of memories to share of his time here and the changes he has seen.

"My life at St Paul's began in November, 1980, soon after we moved to Weston from Hertfordshire because of my work. After trying several churches we came to St Paul's where we immediately felt at home and our two girls were soon singing in the large choir. After several weeks, John Davies asked

Jane and me if we were having our banns read! We pointed out that we had two girls in the choir!

It was not long after this that I was asked to run the youth club, with help from Joan Tapley. It was held on Tuesday nights with 40 – 50 attending and was a lively affair. I particularly remember an outing we went on in 1982, when we took a coach party to visit Wembley Stadium. Looking up the costs for this outing makes interesting reading. Admission was £1-62 for adults and 90p for children. Return coach fare (Bakers) cost £3-50 for adults and £2-50 for children. Those were the days."

(I remember that coach trip well. I didn't go on it myself but Ian went with our young daughter, Esther, and she brought me back a postcard. Rather non-plussed, I asked her why she'd bought a card with nothing but grass on it. "Grass!" she exploded, "That's not just grass! It's the famous Wemberly turf!")

Alan continues, *"There was a very active social life at the church in the eighties, run by a committee. Olive Money was the Cameron Macintosh of St Paul's, writing and producing shows each year for a group called the 'Revellers'. They were desperate one year and asked me to join. I did, found it great fun and made some good friends. Olive gave up producing the shows in 1987 and I took over in 1988. The last show was in 1995 when Huw decided our efforts would be better spent on more important aspects of church life.*

As well as producing shows, I was, for a while, Chairman of the Social Committee. We arranged barn dances, quiz evenings, skittles, trips to the theatre etc. It was a particularly good way of keeping us all together during our time without a vicar."

(It was after one of the skittles evenings, I remember, that Ian and I walked home to find we'd been burgled! Quite a dramatic end to the evening!)

Alan goes on *"I had a heart bypass operation in 2001, (Was it the pressure of those Harvest Supper shows?) but I made a good recovery and returned to work after 6 weeks. The Harvest Supper shows ended and Huw introduced the Alpha Course to St Paul's. Along with Jane, I attended the first course and then went on to lead several Alphas, going with Huw, along with Jane to other churches in Wales and Hertfordshire. We also visited Toronto twice to experience TACE at first hand.*

I became a churchwarden with James Garner in 2004 and we helped Huw to have the pews removed and a new carpet laid, to complete the church decoration in 1997, (during which time the services had to be held in the church hall).

Huw left in 2005, having done a wonderful job at St Paul's and at the end of James Garner's term of office, my wife, Jane joined me as warden. After the interregnum, we were pleased to have our curate, Andrew Alden, take over as Vicar.

I now have less duties. I help to keep the fleet of cleaners working (the machines, not the wonderful group of ladies that clean the church on Monday mornings), and I have various duties at the first service. I am also a member of the Ministry Team, and for a while led a branch group which I still belong to. I have seen tremendous changes at St Paul's in recent years, started by Huw and carried on now, with great vision, by Andrew. As with all changes, to a grumpy old man, some have seemed better than others, but along with Jane, I'm still trying to do my bit."

In Conclusion

A little while ago, when I was vaguely thinking about putting this book together, I was reading 'Be Still and Know', a book on prayer by Michael Ramsey who was Archbishop of Canterbury from 1961 – 1974. He had been describing St Augustine's view of heaven as a 'place' where people will 'rest, see, love, and praise'. Ramsey goes on to suggest that these words, 'rest, see, love and praise', *"tell both of heaven and of the true life of man on earth. They tell no less of the Church's renewal at this and any time. It has been all too possible in the life of the Church for rest to mean a complacently tranquil piety; for seeing to be the seeing of tradition without contemporary awareness, or the seeing of some contemporary enthusiasms without the perspective of history; for loving to be in the circle of the likeable; for praising to be a kind of aesthetic enjoyment. The renewal of the Church will mean, indeed there are signs that it does already mean, a rest which is exposed to the darkness and light.......a seeing of both the heavenly perspective and the distresses of the world, a loving which passes into costly service, and a praising which is from the depth of the soul."*

It struck me as I read the Archbishop's words that St Paul's might today be regarded as one of those places where already 'there are signs' and they are partly the result of all the people who have passed through the church over the last hundred years and worked for it 'in unity', clergy and laiety together. The people of St Paul's who have prayed, loved, cried and laughed together and have always found it in their hearts to say "YES".

And,

"Never once did we ever walk alone

Never once did you leave us on our own

You are faithful, God, You are faithful."